THE WHOLLY SWEDISH EMPIRE

INGEMAR UNGE

THE WHOLLY SWEDISH EMPIRE

Swedes and their pictures

———

TRANSLATED FROM THE SWEDISH
BY
JEREMY FRANKS

SWEDISH TOURING CLUB

SVENSKA TURISTFÖRENINGENS FÖRLAG
FIRST PUBLISHED AS HELSVENSKT © INGEMAR UNGE 1987
TRANSLATED FROM THE SWEDISH BY JEREMY FRANKS
ENGLISH TEXT © SVENSKA TURISTFÖRENINGENS FÖRLAG
DESIGNED BY KJELL LÄHET. COVER PHOTO BY NAN RAUSCHER. DRAWINGS BY BJÖRN BERG
MADE AND PRINTED BY AB FÄLTHS TRYCKERI, VÄRNAMO, SWEDEN 1988
STF PUBLICATION NUMBER 2651
ISBN 91 7156 061-0

When, more than tifty years ago, the Swedish Touring Club organised the first photo competition for its members, they naturally took only black-and-white picturesl. But the result was so successful that STF published a Christmas book of the winning photos and of work by the club's own photographers.

The book and the competition were so well liked that both became annual events, and in the due course a tradition. Motifs were many and varied, and to leaf through the books now is to perceive Sweden afresh—its people, and their surroundings and landscapes.

The tradition continued until 1970. It was resumed in 1979, with colour pictures on the theme of Know Your Own Country, Throughout the Year. While no books have been published, the a winning pictures have appeared in annual calendars, with a picture for each week.

This whole treasure of colour the pictures us the pictures chosen for this book—interesting, informative, beautiful, original pictures, and each in some measure typically Swedish.

We asked Ingemar Unge, whose work in *Dagens Nyheter* has made him one of the best–known humorous writers in Sweden, to consider just what is typically Swedish not just in these pictures but in his observations of Swedes, himself and others, and of our relationship with nature and the natural world. We hope you will enjoy, as we have done, his witty and sympathetic view of some of our idiosyncrasies.

Swedish Touring Club

A gloomy people, much given to merriment.

HJALMAR SÖDERBERG

Here, now, a collection of Swedish images. The choice is in some way typically Swedish, for almost all represent nature: tamed, untamed, dramatic, or cosy, but almost nothing but nature.

For a Swede Sweden is nature.

At what do our *riksdagsmän* stare during their debates in their renovated *riksdag?* A painting of people at work, factories and smoke stacks, cars and houses? No, an enormous tapestry representing the land-and-seascape of the skerries, without a single house or human being in sight.

If asked if there is anything to see in Sweden, the typical Swede would seldom reply Visby, the nuclear power-station Ringhals II, the Old City of Stockholm or the Baltic fishermen's bothies in Västervik, but probably the skerries outside Stockholm, or of the Bohuslän coast or the hospitable desolation of Fårö or Gotska Sandön.

Fårö is quite suitable to boast about to a foreigner because no foreigner may go ashore there without special permission, for the island is designated as militarily sensitive.

A good friend of mine married an American girl and brought her here at the beginning of June.

After about a week she made known that all Swedes were probably crazy, far gone in madness: just about every one of them had congratulated her on having arrived in her new homeland just at the beginning of June when new potatoes would be served on every table.

How in the world could a whole nation have taken leave of their senses about something as prosaic as potatoes? And how could potatoes be the most important reason for visiting Sweden?

'There must be something else to tempt the visitor with?'

'Oh yes,' I said. 'Pickled herrings of various sorts and sour cream and chilled glasses of schnapps, you understand.'

While clearly an improvement on potatoes, this list seemed to this American girl to be merely national propaganda.

But fresh new potatoes are only a symbol of why tourists come here and why Swedes remain here, namely, the few miserable weeks when the ice reluctantly disappears, the snow is replaced by rain, and the sun every now and again tans our pale skins, the weeks during which Swedes come alive and re-live their lives: summer. The Swedish Summer.

It is not just a season in the general meaning of the word, for summer is linked to many components of the Swedish character, to much that a Swede would call typically Swedish.

The Swedish summer is some two months long and a metre deep. Dive into the Baltic, plunge down a few metres, and enter Autumn, lying there in wait, far colder than the surface water. It is as if to receive a reminder of death, suddenly one feels that one's feet are in autumn and winter, that the cold is merely waiting to come up and take over again, like a monster from the depths—no! quickly up to the sun again, it is now summer!

The Swedish Summer is preceded by something called the Swedish Spring, and all its attempts to get across the country's frontiers without attracting notice are doomed to failure.

The shiest and most careful snowdrop, the most farsighted crowfoot, the most cunning colt's foot—none has a chance, for as soon as one of them sends up a shoot some Swede is there and sights them and seizes the phone and rings the papers, which without a moment's doubt write up the matter.

A Swedish editor would not dream of responding: 'Have you lost your wits, woman, to believe this great paper gives a damn about some miserable colt's foot flowering in your garden?'

On the contrary, he makes a careful note of her address and the time and writes a small notice. Such memorialists rarely receive any honorarium, for spreading the news of Spring's progress in our country is a National Duty.

Such progress is called Signs of Spring. The more fanatical observers usually manage to see them towards the end of February. Even un-natural events, such as the opening of the amusement park, Green Glade, in Stockholm, and the like, are accounted Signs of Spring, and it makes no matter if the doors have to be forced open in a howling snowstorm.

Once some event has been accorded the status of a Sign of Spring it cannot be changed.

This business of spring signs is, in fact, of some psychological interest. It is a form of avoidance of reality. One can without

11

difficulty imagine a TV reporter standing in a shower of sleet and snow and saying: 'A sure sign of spring is usually . . .'

It may be children playing ball, or some regularly occuring event, an exhibition, for example. Unbelievable heat, sun and flowers are in themselves not signs of spring, but spring itself. It is the signs that are interesting, proof that spring is springing even if nothing in the natural world suggests this. The flora of un-natural signs of spring are many and rich.

It would actually not be illogical to announce that 'the seventh of May is usually a certain sign of spring . . .' But before we consider the Swedish summer and things to do with it, consider for a moment occurences that can be called typically Swedish. If there are any.

NORMALLY A NATION IS unwilling to label itself or to decide that some characteristics typically distinguish its citizens. That should be left to its surroundings. In his surroundings' eyes a Swede is stupid, 'corked,' to transliterate the word. *Die Dumme Schweden,* say the Germans, who try sometimes to explain it away by saying that the actual expression is *Die dumme Schwebeln,* and applies to some group of domestic fatheads.

Once I owned an American book called *10,000 Jokes, Toasts and Stories.* Its Swedish section featured Swedes, all called Olesen, and all quite unbelievably thick in the head. But the name, Olesen, causes a Swede to suspect some sort of geographical mistake . . . At the same time as the Swede is 'corked,' he lives in one of the most technically advanced countries in the world; a renowned book, *Sweden—The Middle Way,* on the country's already cleverly-managed economy, appeared in the 1930s.

All this doesn't hold together. But what national cliches actually do?

12

The German, for example, is at once the swollen-necked Prussian officer and the confused professor. The Frenchman is an amorous person with ten mistresses, who also devotes himself to a crushingly intense family life; his home is his castle probably to a higher degree than the Englishman's.

Englishmen fight and make trouble in football stadia, full up to the ears with good sportsmanship, jolly good shot, old chap, stiff upper lip, etc, etc, and so on and so on.

After this broadside against national characters, it is perhaps enough to find certain culturally justified characteristics and ask oneself if there are equivalents in other countries.

In general one must decide from which epoch a national cliche comes. A southern Swedish farmhand in New York harbor in 1887 speaking his own odd dialect isn't really to be compared with a solarium-golden representative of Volvo Trucks in Detroit in 1986.

What then is a Swede?

A Swede is a person who never dares to complain that it is too warm; a person who has no idea who wrote either the text or the music to the Swedish national anthem; a person who travels to Italy with two suitcases filled with fish paste, sausage, pickled herring and crispbread to avoid anything foreign during his time abroad. (This is now something from the 1950s and the early 1960s—a modern variant would be a Swede travelling to Italy to see if the pizza is as good as at home in Sweden.)

A Swede is a person who does not know the texts to the songs he considers an irreplaceable part of the Swedish cultural heritage. The very Swedish pastime of community singing degenerates without word sheets into a straightforwardly instrumental entertainment by the resident band.

A Swede is a farmer on a small scale: scrape away one or two generations and a farming surface appears, for up until the mid 1940s, ours was a thoroughgoingly farming country.

A Swede is a person who does as the authorities say. (To this we shall return.)

A Swede is a person who wants to live, at least during summer, with his family in an empty forest, ideally some 150 miles to the nearest farmhouse, but ten metres to the local cooperative store and the state liquor shop. A wilderness, but a civilized one. Mr. Ulf Lundell, poet, novelist and rock singer, has celebrated this in *Open Landscape*—new words in an old melody, which has been proposed as a new national anthem: neighbours should not be seen, and should be audible only when they hold parties.

A human laugh mixed with the cry of a seagull isn't such a bad ideal. In principle, one should be able to go out naked from the house in the early morning to piss onto some bush that had not thought about being anything very special.

That Swedes detest society is a quite common belief among those who detest wildernesses. Jan Myrdal once wrote about a visit to a lighthouse on some rock in the outer skerries.

'But isn't it a little rugged here in autumn?' he wondered.

'Rugged?' replied the lighthouse keeper. 'Have I anything to be afraid of? There's not a person in sight.'

The Swede as hermit. On the other hand, some Swedes pack themselves together willingly in camping places with 10,000 other hermits. Or, as members of the campers' upper class, they do it in caravans, but not as others do it. For them, caravans are to be pulled here and there to allow their owners to see as many new places as possible.

But the Swede, heir of the Vikings, a man of the peat bogs, readily lets his caravan strike root in some camping place, extends it with a tent, fences it all about, arranges a garden of flower boxes and anchors it, turning it into a summer *stuga* on wheels, a home, or at least one in disguise. What can be more delightful, it has been asked in this connection, than striding out of one's caravan in the morning

14

and walking straight into the one parked alongside?

As a farmer and a Viking, a Swede really ought to have a home in the skerries, to best suit his two natures. But houses in the skerries are costly, so whoever wants water near his house must find a place by a lake. We have 100,000 lakes in Sweden.

Hell is a place where Swedes take care of the entertainment, David Frost once said. We aren't much fun: slow-tongued and gloomy, we cry quietly under glimmering birches, overcome with emotion and drink on Midsummer Eve.

Swedes can't manage spirits, say those who can, who believe they form a minority. According to some domestic theoreticians, the majority fumbles after the bottle because its contents cost too much. Another school believes the cause to be that they cost too little.

When Swedes are abroad, according to one prejudice, they try to drink cheap wine in such quantities that, economically, they would have spent the same had they stayed at home and bought the more costly wine on sale in Sweden.

There are many prejudices about Sweden and Swedes. While we don't have more suicides or alcoholics than comparable countries, and while the state doesn't take charge of more children than, for example, it does in England, Swedes go about with a vague feeling that the state pokes its nose into their lives altogether too much.

All-seeing Father State shared that point of view, at least during the years when the bourgeois government was in power, and cast around for something not to care about.

The result was the Friggebo House, the minister of housing of the time being called Friggebo. She and her civil servants decided that any owner of a plot of land intended for a holiday home or the like might, without specific permission, erect almost anywhere on the said plot an additional small building, not exceeding in area ten square metres, to be used to store equipment, as an extra lavatory or the like. All intelligent people equipped theirs with two beds and

15

used it for guests.

UnSwedish mentalities cannot easily understand the limitless gratitude with which this proposal was received by the Swedish people, to whose burdens are added, on average, one new law per hour: it was unique for a paragraph, so to say, to take wing over the sea. I interviewed this minister once: we sat in a lunch bar and were ending our discussion and our lunch when we were approached by a distinguished-looking elderly gentleman. With a voice shaking with emotion he proffered his thanks for this Friggebo House and then, grasping the cabinet minister's hand, he snuffled: 'And one may place the flagpole wherever one will!'

The cabinet minister was almost embarassed to receive this attention, thinking perhaps that the fellow would have done better to have shrieked at her that this Friggebo house was, for God's sake, not enough, that there were one hundred and twenty three other paragraphs that could thrown on the rubbish heap.

In the meantime we are getting off the point: can certain characteristics be justifiably ascribed to a Swede? I asked some foreign friends and they replied promptly.

'A Swede is a person who loudly, not to say formally, tells his company of his intention to go to the lavatory. People of all other nationalities merely take themselves off discreetly: the Swede makes known to all who will listen—usually no-one—that now he's off to the mug, as it's called. No-one ought then to need to wonder where he might have gone or feel obliged to arrange a manhunt or anything equally drastic.

A good friend, resident in London, had provided in his house a tiny cubbyhole in which he kept a handbasin, soap and a small towel. Thither would this sadist direct Englishmen who discreetly wondered where they could wash their hands.

They would quickly emerge again, confused and desperate.

Englishmen today ask directly for the loo.

PHOTO BY EVA OLAUSSON, Trollhättan

A sunny winter day near Trollhättan, with the waters of the Göta River, on the point of freezing, so much warmer than the surroundings that they are steaming. Hardly a sign of spring.
[17]

PHOTO BY ELLA WESTAM, Halmstad

*Some tiny child in goal . . . kids' ice-hockey competitions are taken,
literally, bloody seriously, by grown-ups and children, the latter often
engaging in hand-to-hand argument over the manner of play of their
offspring.*
{18}

PHOTO BY LEIF JÖNSSON, Åkersberga

Those who can manage long-distance skates and dead-smooth Baltic ice may swoop snootily from island to island, over shallows and reefs, landing anywhere, without summer fuss over jetties, mooring lines or anchors.
[19]

PHOTO BY EVA GRANATH, Staffanstorp

*Even Skåne has its winters, snowy and all-too-stormy. Rather like an
avalanche-rescue dog, the householder must nose his way to his own car
rather than his neighbour's before starting to dig.*
[20]

*Huskies have reached Sweden, at least its northern parts, keeping their
original good temper, strength, persistence and obsession with pulling
something.*
{21}

PHOTO BY NAN RAUSCHER, Saltsjö-Boo

PHOTO BY FOLKE SYDVIK, *Göteborg*

*The sign, meaning 'Winter Weather Street,' indicates one of a group of
streets in a Göteborg suburb with 'weather' names: just round the corner
the optimist may find 'Bathing Weather Street.' Like defunct clooks, these
streets get it right once in a while: Spring, Summer, Autumn, Winter,
Thunder, Storm, Cloudy, even Desirable Weather streets wait for the
appropriate occasion . . .*
[22]

One overriding reason why Swedes go even further north, to the fells, in winter: no prepared tracks, just unspoilt natural snow. Recompense enough for long journeys, lift queues and other troubles.
[23]

The Swedish stuga *illustrated (1): this one is at the top of Kebnekaise (just over 2,000m), in a mass of buoyant fleecy cloud that lulls away any sense of great height.*
{24}

Swedes (and others) as lemmings: the starting ritual of Vasaloppet
includes throwing one's excess clothing, in a numbered sack, over a fence.
From 3 $\frac{1}{2}$ to 8 hours later, on arrival in Mora (90 km away) snowy
finishers may reclaim their sacks, which have in the meantime been laid
out in rows in numerical order.

[25]

In the total silence of a forest tarn, someone has managed to lure a pike onto a hook and up through the hole unexpectedly bored through the ice.
[26]

PHOTO BY FREDRIK LAUDON, Malmö

Tired, huddled masses of swans in central Stockholm, enjoying the bounty of the city: piles of bread crusts and the like, charitably renewed daily in winter.
{27}

PHOTO BY KITRI LARSSON, Minnesota

Traditional school building, (de)faced with asbestos cladding and occupied by modern pedagogues. When the bell rings, the pupils emerge and go home on the chairs-on-skates. To use, stand on one runner and kick (spark) *with the free foot, making the vehicle, too, a* spark.
[28]

PHOTO BY BENGT HEDBERG, Solna

Mid-1980s winters have been longer and more snowy than even Swedes can put up with. Snow removal, with grinding motors and flashing lights, is nothing to wake up to, morning after morning.
[29]

Teamwork solves another midwinter crisis. What it was, and how it was solved, was never really clear, even at the time.
[30]

In a rising wind, the snowblind lead the snowblind, with luck, back to the hotel.

[31]

PHOTO BY BIRGITTA BERGSTRÖM, Norrköping

Ice is best either when absolutely new or when old and tired. You stamp on it to see if it will bear, or kick it to give spring a little help.
[32]

As a further example of something quintessentially Swedish, another foreign friend replied: 'Cafes!' She thought them more Swedish than anything, and wholly incomprehensible, for they make use of too many systems.

'Systems?' I said, having not given the matter a thought. 'Each has its own system,' she said. 'So how can one understand which one a cafe makes use of?'

In her view, Swedish cafes can be divided according to their sales methods into four or five principal groups.

In one, the guests sit at table until a waitress comes to ask what one will have. One replies, and in due course she serves it, and one pays her, and consumes it.

In a group-2 cafe one goes first to a counter and chooses what one will eat and then chooses a table. Then a waitress comes to ask what one will drink. She fetches the lot at the counter, and then one pays her.

Elsewhere, one goes first to a counter to choose something to eat, and the assistant wonders what one will drink. One then pays for that, and the eatables, and takes the latter to one's table and then the waitress comes with the coffee or whatever.

In other groups, one pays for the bread at the counter and the coffee at the table, or pays for both coffee and bread at the counter, taking the bread to the table and fetching the coffee from another table set in the middle of the premises.

My foreign lady friend could give an account of three or four other methods, but had never come across in Sweden the Helsinki method: take juice and bread and coffee and consume it all in peace and quiet before accounting to a waitress for the lot; obtain a bill from her; settle it with the cashier.

'It ought to be introduced somewhere in Sweden,' she said. 'So that the list would be complete.'

I reminded myself then that neither the Italian nor the German

33

variant was included: that one goes first to a cashier, says what one wants (without really having any idea of what is on offer), pays, and then takes the receipt to the counter to receive one's cup of coffee.

What more can be said about the Swede?

Earlier it has been suggested that he is shy of people. A knock at the door? His first impulse is to seize an axe, rush out and beat his visitor to death.

How can a visitor be other than an adversary? The ancient Delsbo dialogue supports this interpretation.

'ear, you, 'im over there: 'oo is he?'

'Dunno.'

'Not from these parts, eh?'

'Nay. Shall we do 'im in?'

As a consequence of this imputed shyness, the Swede isn't very hospitable. This isn't really true: things can go rather sluggishly to begin with but, as a Japanese is said to have claimed, getting to know a Swede is like getting ketchup out of the bottle. Nothing at first, nothing afterwards, and then everything all at once in a rush.

I WAS ONCE EXPOSED to hospitality in the north of Sweden, Norrland, together with a photographer, Olle. After a week we were ready for the stiffest possible three-week cure of rice water and breadcrusts.

We had begun at crack of dawn, dragging ourselves out of bed to duck our heads in the lake before making for a hammock, where coffee and buns and dream-cakes and rye-cakes and almond tarts and Danish pastries and wheat cakes and yet some other sort of cake were ready.

34

We set about getting them inside us.

Then we would get up and say our thank you's and try to clear the table, but it would already have been cleared, and the old lady of the house stood in the doorway and asked if we wouldn't like to have a few *smörgås* to take with us, just to make sure. So we made sure with a half-acre of waybread, and eggs and anchovies.

'I've put on more coffee,' said the old lady.

(In Norrland coffee's on the stove day and night.)

And all time people came and went in the kitchen, and helped themselves and poured out and chewed and talked about elks and what the devil's the matter now with the Evinrude again, and have you fixed the door, and the dog's got onto the road again, and is there some coffee?

And now be sure you take enough, we don't want you going hungry.

We staggered out and met the old man of the house who said that lunch would soon be ready but have a couple of *smörgås* each if you like. Making our thanks at a half run across the lawn, the hiss of air entering a vacuum pack of coffee at our backs, Olle and I hid ourselves in our caravan, sitting staring blankly before us, trying to look occupied as relatives stick their heads in to say that coffee's ready.

Then we have lunch.

We have sweet fruit drinks and milk and sour milk and well-prepared sandwiches and slices of veal with potatoes served with a four-litre bucket of bearnais sauce, and herrings and beer and cheese and bread and salad. The old lady purrs contentedly in a corner, the stove glows, people come and go all the time, everyone stands, talking about a cafe they visited in Stockholm, and how Anita and her husband will be here soon, and what the devil, hasn't the dog got onto the road again? Shouldn't we fetch a little more to drink from the storeroom? Won't you help yourself to a little more, go on, don't be so shy about it, we don't want to have to feed the meat to the dogs, no, no, come along now, one must have enough to eat, have you tried the herring?

Olle and I ran away. We crept away between the birches down by the road, and walked towards the bridge. When we got there we found the old man waiting with his boat. 'I saw you went off for a walk, listen to me, you boys, you must be tired and ought to get home, I've got a lifejacket here, if you take the painter, I've got coffee,'

His wife, lively and rosy cheeked, said she had made a few *smörgås*—seemingly about ten thousand of them, with prawns—and then Olle and I tried to walk round the place until dinner time. We managed four circuits.

Before eight kilos of spare ribs and a shot of schnapps, as clear as water, and sweet fruit drinks and milk and beer and *smörgås,* and do come along now and show what your appetites are, you men. People talk all the time, the *stuga* is bursting, and then we have coffee and dream-cakes, and tosca-cakes and golden vanilla sauce . . . and stagger out and lie down in the caravan and stare up to its roof. About one in the morning a cautious knocking on the window heralds the old man, whispering of bowls of strawberries in the kitchen.

Afterwards we wondered how the members of this family didn't all weigh about 400 pounds apiece, but they didn't.

Well, now, we have at last a National Poet who acquired his resoundingly elevated title well within living memory. His name is Evert Taube.

All cultured nations have long had National Poets, but Sweden had no-one until recently: Carl Mikael Bellman hadn't really coped, and Heidenstam was a national poet principally for those who intensively wished that Sweden should have one.

But national poets, and personal nicknames, cannot be consciously designated: anything of that sort must come about by itself. Even so, one wonders if Sweden, so ancient in some ways, is otherwise so youthful that its national poet grew to adulthood first during the late twentieth century?

And what could one say about that?

Sweden, naturally a latent People's Home ever since the mists of time began to dissipate over Uppsala or wherever, had still to wait until the 1930s, when Per Albin Hansson, and social minister Möller, and the Saltsjöbadet Agreement, could mould the frame in which to hang the portrait of a national poet, once we had one. With State Liquor Stores systematically established and Sickness Compensation and legal rights to paid holidays secured, the Swedish Nation was ready to press some National Poet to its breast.

It chose Evert.

He made his calm entry, with his great genius, when the time was ripe. He appeared and saved our country's honour among nations, for a national poet is the right of any self-respecting nation.

He became a bard in blue and gold, and blue and gold he remains, however much he may sing of the pampas and Liguria.

I recall an occasion in 1968. Evert Taube was to sing at Green Glade (known to Swedes as *Gröna Lund*); but as he was getting on a bit, the planned, rehearsed confusions were becoming more and more frequently mixed with the real thing. His voice became hoarse, and so did his lute playing. The place was packed.

I had taken along an American street musician, Ken, who stood there in jeans, carrying an 88-string guitar, amazed that twenty-seven thousand people had packed themselves in there in the light rain to listen to an old man mumble from one microphone to another. The public's love reached compactly all the way up to Evert,

37

and the American couldn't avoid feeling it.

People joined in and sang and helped. Everyone wanted to hear him sing 'My darling you are like a rose,' his adaptation of Burns' classic verse.

It was then that I saw that Evert Taube had saved the face of the Swedish nation among the countries of the world by becoming our national poet.

Swedes often scold each other, quite unreasonably, for lacking soulfulness, cultural interests and a feeling for tradition. Take the theatre, for example. We have in fact a theatre public that is much larger than those for either football or ice hockey. Stockholm has many more theatres per capita than London, for example, which does not precisely lack stages.

This interest in the theatre finds expression in acting, too. We have a mass of locally-set plays in which Swedes unite their interest for the theatre with concern for their home tracts and traditions.

Locally-set plays have a certain degree of conformity in their plots: the farmer on a large scale, the forestry company or nasty-minded bailiff threatening some brave indignantly honourable smallholder, an angry father to put a spoke in the wheel of Young Love over the Farm Boundary. The smallholder maintains his stand, the young lovers continue to clasp one another, and as a rule both the father and the bailiff relent in the end. Honour and the honest emerge victorious.

The play of this sort I know best, *The People of the Stony Coast,* is performed annually on Öland. By and large the same company plays it each year. A compelling figure with a pointed beard and a voice like granite declaims a highly formal prologue, full of stones, our fathers' lands, wind, sun and water. It celebrates honourable conduct and steadfast friendship.

The patriachial master mason speaks with his patriarchially honourable relatives about how the right has finally been acquired to trade freely from Öland, without the obligation to sell to the grasping merchants of Kalmar, who scarcely favour the farmers of Öland.

The master mason, sound as his own stones, is to journey to the castle of Borgholm to meet the prince, a fine honourable man. With his honourable guest the mason drives off to meet the honourable prince, and their meeting goes as might be expected. Neither disappoints the other and they reach agreement.

Then all good men gather at the mason's and drink his good beer, and the only person who cannot see the beauty of it is of course the pastor, a fine example of a hated Lutheran prelate, who detects the Devil's reeking anus in anything that could murmur of the people's good. But the people ignore him, as they have anyway ignored his domesday sermons of forthcoming cupidity and thrift among the farmers.

There is something confidingly moving about all these honourable people who populate our local plays, which breathe a liberating belief in righteousness and a sense that justice will sooner or later be rewarded.

Ancient male achievements are especially prominent in these plays. Their tones ring out in diverse Swedish films from the 1930s, the time of the breakthrough of democracy, where straight-backed men in black waistcoats announce that the Swedes are masters in their own house now, and other more or less bombastic things, because the Social-Democratic Party has won and Per Albin leads the government.

Swedish males like to see themselves as men of their word, blonde and sure-handed at the rudder of some sturdy boat, braving the waves of the North Sea.

WHAT MORE IS THERE that can be taken for granted about Swedes and Sweden? The cook book published by the National Social Board, perhaps: its authors make heroic but scarcely successful attempts to turn their schoolmasters' rods into conjurers' wands.

Busybodies one and all, and so typical of Swedish authority, they try to make something pleasantly unnecessary into something necessarily unpleasant: 'Food that has been fried too hard is neither good nor nourishing,' they claim, heedless of the delights of crisp pork chops and bacon. And by page 35 they drop their guard to proclaim baldly that 'food containing flour, grains, spaghetti and macaroni is nourishing, cheap and good to eat.' 'Taking exercise—that's fun' they cry out, only to make known later that 'a glass of water on arising in the morning feels fine.'

This nervous iron-fisted meddlesomeness! Who is surprised when they are disbelieved, for in what they say they sound like a workhouse caterer or a dessicated maiden aunt scolding a four-year-old nephew. Their I-know-better-than-you-do tone is heard also in the wording of our road signs.

'Stop! Not applicable when driving onto the ferry.' This command may be read by any car ferry over river or lake or between islands in the skerries. Its author must have been so impressed with himself, and the authority of his sign, that he felt the qualification was necessary. But would any motorist drive on board the ferry if it were lacking?

A sort of traffic light without lights and colours, it expresses also the bureaucrat's eternal confidence that without me, dear people, you would perish in distress. Might not the sign read: 'Wait here until it is time to drive on board'?

A good friend of mine tussled with the National Highway Authority over a sign, and won. He had nailed up a bit of wood on the roadside by his summer place, Gulltorpet, and painted its name on it, to guide his friends and acquaintances. The Man from the

Authority informed him that no sign might have such an appearance, and if one were absolutely necessary, it would have to be a sign of prescribed size, and form, and colour, and of the prescribed metal plate. And if not there would be fines.

Such a sign would cost him a couple of thousand *kronor*, or rather more than he wanted to pay to ensure his friends came to his summer party, but he had no wish to pay fines, either. Instead he made a very large wooden letterbox inscribed, in large red letters, with the name of his place, and, in rather smaller white letters, with his own name, Andersson.

Signs fall within the responsibility of the National Highway Authority, which cares nothing at all for letterboxes, for which the Post Office, if anybody, feels responsible. All are now happy.

A foreign friend once became a little confounded on seeing one of the signs in the Stockholm *tunnelbana* that absolutely prohibit dogs and other furred animals from entering or being taken into certain carriages, lest passengers with allergies to furred animals be discomforted. The prohibition is, however, qualified: 'Not applicable to guide dogs.' My foreign friend wondered to whom this sentence is addressed. 'Hardly the blind or even any of their guide dogs, for however skilfully trained they may be, these beasts have yet to learn to read.'

'To a Friend of Good Order,' I said. 'A paragraph-demented person who would most likely throw out the blind man and his dog if he encountered them in some other carriage.' But my friend replied that if one is attempting to spare the allergic the presence of dogs surely even guide dogs ought to be excluded, lest an allergic person find a dog making up to him.

'He would be everyone's friend becomes no-one's friend,' as Queen Christina said.

41

Worry over discrimination makes this prohibition of animals ineffectual, so that an allergic person cannot really feel safe anywhere, even if guide dogs are not a very common sight.

And anyway, there are other laughable signs.

Outside military establishments they announce that persons may absolutely not enter the area nor do so while having explosives or a camera in their possession. Spies and dynamite-carrying saboteurs thus commit two crimes at once: as if blowing the whole place up is not enough, they also offend the rule which prohibits them from entering the place to do so.

Yet another sign that's good for a laugh is the one that's usually to be seen beneath or close to the one that prohibits motor vehicles on a road. The second sign reads: 'Not applicable to vehicles with permission.'

Here, too, one asks oneself: for whom is this sign intended? Hardly the driver of a vehicle with permission, for example, the driver of a refuse truck, who would be well aware of his permission and thus entitled to ignore any prohibition of this sort.

And those who don't have permission to use the road would scarcely be pleased to be reminded that there are others who do. Those without permission need know only one thing: that they are not welcome here.

That someone builds a road only to forbid all traffic from using it is not something that anyone believes, it must be clear that some vehicles with special permission have right of way. I have always thought that the sign should be re-formulated to read: 'Vehicles that may enter here, may enter here.' This, at least, is what I understand the sign actually to mean, nor is there anything to be said against its logic.

The prize for excessively logical signs would be won, however, by any of the fantastic signs saying NOT UP (or NOT DOWN) which are to be seen in the Stockholm *tunnelbana*. They are, in fact, very sensible, probably being formulated by a philosophical sort of sign maker for the fussy traveller who is also plagued with the over-developed sense of order that demands labels on everything.

At the foot of an escalator that comes rolling down towards you from above, you are confronted with the phenomenon of an Escalator That Moves Neither Up Nor Down (in relation to you). This might be called the Duke of York's Paradox (from the children's rhyme, of course), but lest it hold you in thrall, and delay your arrival at work, the Stockholm Local Traffic Board (SLTB, or *SL* in Swedish) has a sign reading NOT UP. This is quite or almost correct: it ought to be complemented with the words NOT DOWN, or, better still, be re-phrased to read NEITHER UP NOR DOWN.

But this would be dangerous, drawing attention to the paradox, and failing to prevent the overthoughful traveller from confusion about the direction in which the escalator actually does move. Confusion must at all costs be avoided.

So, at the top of an escalator that moves up towards one, since it goes neither down nor up, SLTB has a sign reading NOT DOWN (*EJ NED*), sound proof of the care it devotes to its passengers. Other countries' underground systems content themselves with signs read-ing UP or DOWN, or simply don't bother at all: their passengers have to cope on their own in an unSwedish chaos, fighting their way up downward escalators, or down upward ones, all the time bump-ing into fortunate travellers who have managed to get on the right one.

One of my relatives found a sign in California—WRONG ROAD—standing at the supposed entry to a one-way road properly only entered from its other end. Stockholmers will be reminded of the legendary sign, DRIVE WITH CARE, ONE-WAY ROAD IN THE OPPOSITE DIRECTION, a product of students of the Techni-cal College, and their bi-annual magazine, *Gåsblandaren,* as it is called in autumn.

MANY SWEDISH SIGNS TRY to disclaim responsibility of some sort.

Building sites, for example, display copies of an idiotic sign reading: 'Parents who allow their children to play on this site are responsible for any damage caused.' Is there a single Swedish parent who leads his kids to a building site, abandoned on a Sunday, and says: 'Look! Isn't this just the playground you've been looking for?'

And if any twelve-year-old gets into a building site and mangles one of the cranes with his teeth, doesn't he do it, to one hundred percent, without the knowledge and consent of his parents?

And whoever puts up such signs knows this very well, and merely pretends that parents of teenage kids have nothing to do but follow their children about 24 hours a day.

When a building is being renovated, it happens quite often that the sidewalk or pavement, and sometimes half the roadway, is blocked by scaffolding and planks, whereupon someone puts up a sign: 'Pedestrians are directed to the other side of the road.' What amazing good fortune! They might otherwise remain standing, for weeks, in front of the planks, until work on the site is finished.

The Swedish busybodiness is reflected from time to time in our signs.

I said earlier that Swedes do as the authorities say, and foreigners who come here are amazed at our obedience, and see only conformity and subservience all about them.

Of Germans it has been said that they cannot storm a railway station without first obtaining platform tickets, and of Swedes that they cannot make a revolution, for revolutions are forbidden.

Here, again, these cliches don't add up. Of Sweden, a centrally-directed socialistic nation, the foreign media report regularly that the country is friendly to commercial and industrial business enterprise over which, in addition, a handful of families exercises an astonishingly large influence.

We seem to be extraordinarily pleased, while sitting on two chairs at once, to look as if we are actually sitting on only one. In the process our politics lose something of their sting: the *riksdag* has a political scale from left to right, but the Russians see everyone sitting on the right, but when the Americans take a look the whole bunch seems to have moved over to the left, where they sit around and try to find something to debate.

With central direction there follows, inescapably, a powerful bureaucracy, but in that respect Sweden is neither unique nor worst.

The bureaucracies of Tsarist Russia or Soviet Russia must be hard to outdo, likewise that of Prussia, while Bakunin (or was it Kropotkin?) once complained that were a tree to fall across a road in France, no fewer than fourteen official persons, from different levels, would have to formulate decisions before it might properly be sawn up and removed.

With bureaucracy comes an incomprehensible language that common citizens have difficulty in understanding, but even here Sweden is not unique, despite alarms about leaden-footed paragraph-sized lumps of Swedish supplied by their authorities.

The following is an attempt to translate the original Swedish of a notice about something:

"With reference to paragraph 2, section IV, of the minutes of the meeting of 20 April, and according to a decision made by the management group, those persons, who perform such services to which access can be said to be adequate and intended to promote contact such as that indicated in the paragraph and decision referred to above, are hereby invited to a general introduction to, and practical exercises concerning, the preparation of pro memoria, general communications in writing, or pronouncements for the benefit of private persons or legal entities, in such a way that any recipient's acceptance of the cognitive burden of

45

the said pro memorium, communication in writing or pronouncement directed to an individual or corporate person, promulgation of a decision made by this administration or the like be such as is provided in paragraph 2 above. Auditorium C. All are welcome!''

A careful reading of this text may reveal that the original had been an invitation to a course in Auditorium C on the art of writing intelligibly to members of the public to which, however, no-one came, not even the person who was to hold it.

But this meaningless bureaucratic language is by no means only a Swedish phenomenon. Once upon a time an American found a couple of cans of paint in his cellar and, thinking to use them to paint his sauna, he wrote, for safety's sake, to some Federal expert on poisons and asked if the paint in question might be used in a warm, damp place such as a sauna.

The expert replied accordingly but incomprehensibly, ending his letter with the sentence that 'the risk of intoxication in the premises in question is likely to be considerable.' His questioner replied, with thanks for this helpful advice, saying that he had written in the first place because, wanting to paint his sauna yellow, he had had the good luck to find these two cans of yellow paint just when he needed them! The expert answered in an irritated letter in which he repeated what he had already written, only to get the answer that, thanks very much, he had understood the whole thoroughly and it was all as clear as daylight for him, but this time the expert's patience ran out, and he wrote, what he might well have written first: 'For God's sake, don't paint your sauna with that paint, at so high a temperature it'll give off poisonous fumes!'

But Swedes are certainly plagued by bureaucratic language, not least during the time of year for tax returns or in regulations concerning traffic, for example. The regulations of the weight of trailers and the permitted speeds, in relation to their weights, at which they may be drawn, are celebrated examples of what can

46

confuse even the most bureaucratically arranged intellect. And stories of bureaucratic rigidity from the newspapers are innumerable, with plentiful examples of newly-born citizens being subjected to demands, backed up by threats of distraint, for payment of back taxes.

If one really wishes to sample the indignation of Swedes over matters of this sort the correspondence columns of, in particular, daily papers in the north of the country are full of rage over Jack-in-office-Sweden, its authorities and their bureaucratic terror. A young man outside Örnskjöldsvik, in Ångermanland (a little more than half way up Sweden on the right-hand side): 'Yes, you know, once you could arrange a dance on a Saturday night, put two fiddle players on a plank, let people bring coffee with them, or schnapps, but now, Oh my God, no-one dares to think of arranging a dance—you have to have specially-trained guards with walktie-talkies, and lavatories for the handicapped, and police permission, and royalties to the Musicians' Union, and papers, and controllers and the devil knows what, they've ruined simple pleasures here with their shit.'

S WEDEN IS A COUNTRY organised through-and-through, of that there's no doubt, and the language of administrators spreads via TV to Swedes who, whenever they have occasion to appear on the box, exhibit a remarkable conformity in their manner of saying what they want to say. Anyone at all gets muddled in front of a camera and starts "weighing up remedies" and "formulating decisions" and the like.

It is a bit tempting to look backwards in time, and try to explain our civil servants' strong position and centralisation with reference to Swedish history, for there do seem to be certain elements in it which are specifically Swedish.

We have, for example, never had any real feudalism in the country and so no really impressive conflict between the aristocracy and the monarch.

Our shining lights ever since Gustav II Adolf's days at the start of the early modern period, in Europe, at least, have not been stiff-necked landowners and upstarts, but civil servants and administrators. The highest offices were for centuries a preserve of the nobility which thus put itself forward as servants of the king.

When we were Catholics the church was not merely a long way off, geographically, from Rome. When Gustv Wasa, roughly Henry VIII's contemporary, decided we were all to be Protestants the matter was settled without convulsions, mass emigration, riots, or protests. It was about as peaceful and orderly as the change, in 1967, from left-hand driving to right-hand driving.

The strongly individualistic element of the Renaissance seems to have missed us, too, so much so that even such a disturber of the peace as Strindberg tells off an egocentric Renaissance figure in one of his historical novels.

Sweden has never been occupied nor been the meeting point of population movements back and forth across Europe. Our language has never been exposed to any particularly powerful foreign influence but has kept its roots all the time well nourished in the same deep Germanic humus. The Swedish state church has always been so intimately linked with central state power that the village pastor has always been accepted as a person in authority among bailiffs and sheriffs. As recently as the first decade of this century bishops were, as ephors, the supreme supervisors of grammar schools.

And Swedish pastors held their crosses at the wrong end, more like swords than anything else; it was only towards the end of the nineteenth century that we acquired anything at all like full freedom to exercise religious belief.

We have actually had one general strike, and, although it ended

48

Something regal in the woodpile: an ermine (Mustela erminea). Its summer pelt is brown.
[49]

PHOTO BY THOMAS ANDERSSON, Falkenberg

*Cranes migrating through Sweden stop to 'dance' and pair at Hornboga
Lake, midway between Stockholm and Göteborg, around which potatoes
are grown, literally, for the birds.*
[50]

*A 'sign of spring' is sprigs of birch prinked with dyed feathers and hawked
for sale, here outside the Concert Hall in Stockholm.*
[51]

PHOTO BY SVENERIK LINDMAN, Falun

One of the few wild flowers with which we are on botanical first-name terms, Tussilago farfara. It often establishes itself on freshly bulldozed soil, and flowers in very early spring.
[52]

The stars of innumerable TV nature-films, cock and hen capercailles pair off with strip-cartoon clucks, hisses, pops and whispers.
[53]

PHOTO BY LENNART SANDSTRÖM, Norrköping

The Swedish stuga *illustrated (2): a red-and-white one is an essential element in Swedish summer dreams of messing about with old stones and old wood.*
[54]

Easter and May Day fires are to encourage the sun to return. The worshippers stand around at a suitable distance, like bronze-age shadows.
[55]

PHOTO BY BROR JOHANSSON, Avesta

Perhaps a model for a weather vane, but actually wood cutting with a belt-driven saw.
[56]

Swedish paradise: hay, a scythe, a roosting hen, and the cackle of other free hens outside in the sun.
{57}

PHOTO BY FREDRIK LAUDON, Malmö

In the park with the kids, who try to count the ducklings, and the grown-ups wonder how the ducklings have escaped seagulls, pike and foxes.
[58]

PHOTO BY ROLF NYSTRÖM, Hölö

Fox hunting.
[59]

PHOTO BY KJELL STRÖMNER, Stenungsund

Help! A bird has perched upon me! I love birds, but this is going too far.
[60]

Grass and other roots rustle and snuffle and grow and scratch and crawl with life, once one has got down to them.
[61]

PHOTO BY BENGT AF GEIJERSTAM, Stockholm

Fiddle players are increasing in numbers: they originate as young bearded men with open looks, long medieval-trimmed hair, black mushroom-shaped hats, black waistcoats and curly-toed leather boots. They and their audiences find years of delight in the traditional melodies.
[62]

Urban traditions include country-style weddings: this one was celebrated in Enskede, a Stockholm suburb.
[63]

PHOTO BY LARS-ERIK INGDÉN, Älvsjö

*Baptism, as here, in a shieling and in traditional country dress, confirms
or establishes country roots.*
[64]

PHOTO BY STIG EDVARDSSON, Norrköping

Three reindeer in the highlands of Sarek National Park. Excepting only Lapps, people here feel a little out of place, and diminished, by such unusually large-scale nature.
{65}

PHOTO BY LARS DAHLSTRÖM, Insjön

Stallions in spring. Once again a common sight in the Swedish country-side, horses are cherished, but not for the ancient Northern pastime of horse fighting.
{66}

A Tengmalm's Owl (Aegolius funereus), with prey. 'Owls eat rodents,' say the schoolbooks, but only TV has brought home what red-in-tooth-and-claw, eat-and-be-eaten, and food chains mean to those most closely involved.
{67}

PHOTO BY INGMAR RESLEGÅRD, Uppsala

The Swedish stuga *illustrated (3): an interior. Here a fishing net is to be laid as nets have been laid, time out of mind. And one fishes, not for the pot, but as a rite, a pleasure, a tradition . . .*
{68}

A hobby fisherman puttering out early to lift the net he laid last night . . . his sleepy son unaware that he'll appreciate the net of wriggling fish, and the smells and sounds of the morning, first when he's adult. The shadows are of the bridge that connects Öland with the mainland: to determine its length, count the lamp-posts and multiply by about 20 metres. Or ask at the tourist office . . .
{69}

PHOTO BY GÖTE ERIKSSON, Trollhättan

PHOTO BY GÖSTA SKOGLUND, Göteborg

A final in the Insjöhus Cup for young people. The girl on the right may have forgotten her running shoes, but has managed to win in stockinged feet.
[70]

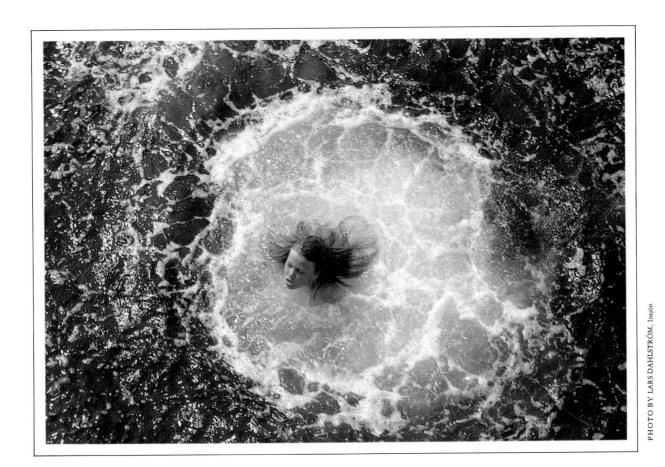

PHOTO BY LARS DAHLSTRÖM, Insjön

*Summer bathing in the sea, kids staying in so long that they get wrinkled
and blue, and never get out*
[71]

PHOTO BY INGMAR HELLSTRÖM, Hedemora

Bailing after the first launch, or in preparation of a day's fishing, or a stretch along the reed beds.
[72]

In the country, water is fetched by bucket and washing is done by hand, say men, who know what real country traditions are.
[73]

PHOTO BY LENNART FLOOD, Göteborg

PHOTO BY LARS FORSNER, Stora Skedvi

A little music on the side, perhaps during a football half-time break. Brass bands are otherwise part of a Swedish health-spa tradition that includes guests parading four-by-four preceded by triangle-playing children, wind instruments, and banners.
[74]

PHOTO BY BROR JOHANSSON, Avesta

Traditions in combination: community singing and local costume.
[75]

PHOTO BY LENNART BROBORN, Trollhättan

*A tiny person from a big city in a larger landscape where a human life is
easily swallowed by its longer, slower rhythms.*
[76]

*Swedish summer, at most two months long and a meter deep, and too often
inviting in inverse proportion to one's degree of clothing.*
[77]

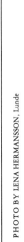

Not *Guinness-book pizza, but traditional Swedish crispbread: thin, brittle and floury, and very traditional, very.*
[78]

A little crooked chair and a wall of crumbling plaster are bits of summer delights, and in their place, in the country. The chair would land in the nearest skip, in town: maybe it came from one.
[79]

Swedish summer, with rain, car, and red stuga. *The rain, if violent, should be not more than enough for the grass and the potato patch, and allow time for tea and a hand of cards inside.*
[80]

with the defeat of the workers, it did give both sides something to think about. Since then the labour market has been a place of compromises longed for and attained, where a disciplined broad outlook from both its parties has preserved a remarkable peace. The closeness of the trade-union movement, *LO* (*LandsOrganisation*), to the Social-Democratic party, and so to effective political power for some fifty years, has had something to do with this. Only recently have strikes once again become frequently-used weapons.

The entire process of industrialisation was carried through in Sweden without excessively large convulsions in the body of society.

A contributory factor has perhaps been the very special 'works' phenomenon—water-powered industrial undertakings usually way off in the forests, but (still the case) with customers far beyond the country's frontiers: perhaps the most celebrated was the early seventeenth-century de Geer enterprises, suppliers of cast-iron cannon in batches of up to several hundred at a time. The 'works' were organised, however, rather like large-scale agricultural centres.

One of the first de Geer's contemporaries, Axel Oxenstierna, was not only Sweden's deservedly most renowned administrator, but one of Europe's, too. Ennobled by Queen Christina, he had previously been right-hand man (and left, too, at times) to her father, Gustav II Adolf. Among his many creations the Buildings Board (*Byggnadsstyrelse*) has retained its name and power up to the present; it stills allows the state to keep a very close eye on every aspect of building in the country.

I remember from school how we had rather mixed feelings about such figures as the poet Runeberg's county chancellor—the man obliged to receive the conquering Russian after the catastrophes in Finland in 1809, but who, Swedish statute book in hand, admonished him, at his peril, to respect the laws of Sweden even in the future. There, we were to think, was a real Swedish administrator, a man who so loved his laws and regulations that he would bow to the power that would enforce them and maintain him at his duty of keeping intact the sacred paragraphs, of penning the holy script, and recording the timeless minutes.

The question of the peasant-like subordination of the Swede to heavy-footed authority, and his—or her—relationship to nature are connected: when Swedes revolt their uprisings have had something to do with nature. Some few years ago it concerned the elms of *Kungsträdgården,* the pleasant little park in the centre of Stockholm that had been left largely undisturbed by the blitz-like destruction of half the old centre of the city. It was announced that the elms were to be felled to build an entry to a new *tunnelbana* station. This was altogether too much.

A dazed flock of local politicians were faced with their hitherto conveniently docile charges scrambling up into the elms, and roosting there by night, to hinder any attempt to fell them; with a blizzard of flysheets over Stockholm's Venetian *Stadhus;* with meetings agitating in almost permanent session; and with a most unSwedish air of carnival over the entire scene. The man who would have been called Mayor in the Anglo-Saxon world, Hjalmar Mehr, a Social-Democrat politician, and his colleagues, tried to laugh the whole thing off as mere street democracy by 'activists,' irresponsible youth, dubious elements, . . . but this cut no ice.

At a meeting called by the city fathers, one urban patriarch asked an elderly man in the crowd who he might happen to be, but learned from the angry reply—'von Döbeln!'—that here was a descendant of the legendary Swede who had defied in turn the Russians, the Norwegians, the Emperor Napoleon, and, for good measure, his own king, too, not to mention a death sentence for insubordination, and a musket bullet in the head. Clearly, the opposition was not merely a gang of unemployed street toughs. So he, and other gentlemen in tailored overcoats, and hippies with flowing locks, vegetarian environmentalists and formidable ladies in pudding-basin hats continued to mount guard over the elms.

This cross section of the whole city proved irresistable, and impervious to heavy-father rhetoric about parliamentary principles, the fundamentals of representative democracy (the prevailing system in Sweden), responsibility, good order, good working conditions and traditions. The city fathers received a polite hearing. They were then told that no-one gave a damn for principles without elms.

The trees were to remain, being part of surrounding that were not to be changed. Trees cannot be moved, unlike entries to (or exits from) underground systems. The city fathers put their heads together and produced a gardener: 'These elms are so sick and rotten and disease-ridden that they may fall at any minute. It is a work of charity to put them out of their misery without delay.' It was then that Stockholmers began to find a well-grounded distrust of experts; it blossomed wonderfully some years later, during debates on nuclear energy policy.

The trees did remain, some other place was found for the entry (or exit), nor could the principles of democracy be invoked to reach a decision that offended the greater part of the people of Stockholm. It would have been as ridiculous as the meeting recorded in the minute that read: 'With the exception of the chairman, the members of the committee voted against the decision.'

Those sick elms still stand, people still drink tea and coffee under them in summer, and Karl XII still stands, pointing the unfamiliar visitor to the Grand Hotel, and still enduring the attentions of the pigeons.

A further good example of Swedish revolt are the happenings on the west coast, not far from the frontier with Norway, some miles inland from the coast, where a moorland site was selected, in Stockholm, to be tested as a possible repository for nuclear wastes. This is Kynnefjäll. A gang with drilling and other machinery arrived there in 1980. Their instructions were, in effect, to drill so many test holes into the bedrock that it would become useless for its intended purposes.

But not a hole was bored. A hundred people from the neighbourhood sat down on the road and the drilling crew had to retire. Since April 1980 the neighbourhood has kept watch over its moors, day and night throughout the year, nor will they give up until they receive a written assurance from the government that all plans for waste disposal there have been abandoned.

The neighbourhood has in fact put up a *stuga* for the lookouts, helped by one of the farmers, Erik Johansson, who has provided land and water; of course the *stuga* has white-painted corners.

And the look-outs keep their twelve-hour watches: looking out over the rocky moors, studying, knitting, reading, writing up the diary in the *stuga*.

'It's here we live,' said Erik Johansson. 'It's here we have our roots, and it's here our future is. We don't want atomic rubbish spoiling it.'

So much for that.

His brusque words remind one of the village leader in Ornolac, Sabarthes, in the south of France, a stiff-necked medieval figure: 'The tithes that the bishop demands may well be in accordance with general law, but the inhabitants are right to oppose them, for they are contrary to their own customs.'

The people of Kynnefjäll have said Enough in the face of what is claimed to be development. They refer to their traditions; one of them said: 'We haven't inherited the earth from our parents. We have borrowed it from our children.'

This is only too true. A feeling for their environment is very great.

A SWEDISH CHILD, on being asked to draw a house, will draw a red house with white-painted corners, with a flagpole with a Swedish flag blowing in one direction, and with chimney smoke blowing away in the other.

According to Swedish assumptions, a house is the same as an ancient farm *stuga*—that's what's meant by a home. 'Childhood home' doesn't mean the eight-storey block in a suburb where one spent one's childhood, but a little red *stuga* against a background of shining dark conifers.

That's a Swedish home.

One of the attractions of Stockholm is Skansen, where numbers of old farm buildings and farms have been re-erected. Skansen is visited annually by a couple of million Swedes (out of a total population of 8m). Most of them live in modern apartments, modern semi-detached houses, or modern free-standing houses. When they stoop their way into these low timber-built buildings it is with the feeling that this is how one really ought to be living.

Not that there is anything wrong about their homes, they probably offer everything that one needs in the way of comfort and convenience, but at the same time they aren't really quite right.

All these modern Swedes—plastics engineers, computer experts, communications workers, dockers and stevedores, business-administration graduates—respectfully finger the many worn pieces of equipment and tools, think about how they were made, try to imagine children playing on the broad planks of the floor, compute the comfort coefficient of the open fireplace, pat the walling of the chimney piece, and get under the skin of generations of farmers and smallholders.

In the same spirit, many Swedes demand so much of their summer places: newly-built sport *stugor,* isolated or in planned developments, or some do-it-yourself construction, but ideally some old fisherman's bothy in the skerries or a farm from the early nineteenth century, where they can go about in the farmyard and commune with all the mass of previous owners, farmers and small-holders. Part of the ideal is to close the outhouse door with its aged burnished hand-forged hook, to shut the cart-shed door on the new Volvo 740 with some bone-hard wooden fastening, to lock up by setting a clumsy old billet of wood against the outer door.

The floor ought to glow with the patina of centuries of scouring, the iron stove to shine with blacking, its hood whitened with some chalky wash—in brief, each time one grips a handle or lever it must be to clasp anew some of the thousands of invisible hands from the past that now bind the new owner into the same long tradition, a link in the great chain of time.

'Yes, they knew what they were doing, those farmers,' says the computer director, pleased with the neat closure to the cart-shed door.

Stig Claeson is an author whose work is often characterised by a sort of pleasant melancholy, and it is the melancholy of the half-abandoned countryside that is perhaps his principal theme in *Who Loves Yngve Frej?* At one point in the book there is concern over a wooden scythe pole which had cow horns as handles; they were smooth and their curves fitted the hands comfortably.

A city couple want to buy the pole, but the old men on the farm can't understand why. For them the pole is only part of a tool—and worthless by itself; for city folk it is a cult object, redolent with tradition, work and their ancestry in a farming land.

If one wants to arrange an exhibition in Sweden that will be a sure-fire success, it should concern old-fashioned hand crafts; exhibitions with improbable titles like "Old-fashioned embroidery" or "Stitches that have been used" or "Splitting roof shingles" and so on attract astonishingly large crowds. Something of the sort won Liljevalchs, the Stockholm gallery near Skansen, one of their biggest successes: people queued in rain and sleet to get in.

This fantastic interest doesn't concern just a compulsion to preserve the past, but has something to do with our present too. But what present?

As the here-and-now always is, ours is untranquil, complicated, difficult to comprehend. On top of that, we live in a society of experts, and everyday most of us use equipment that we know only how to use; if anything goes wrong we can't even cobble together a plausible explanation, or a suggestion of how to fix it. So when environmental pollution disturbs our senses, and OPEC's pricing policy immediately influences our standards, naturally it's a relief to get back to something we can really do, ourselves.

I know a highly-placed civil servant who works only part-time and devotes the rest of her time to such hand crafts. She can spend over fifty hours making a little basket from birch-tree roots that can't be used for anything, except perhaps to hold buttons or ten *öre* coins (the smallest now in use, and not used very much), but it is a very fine little basket, regular in form and doesn't topple over. For her it is worth every one of her fifty hours: she has made it all by herself, it has been both journey and arrival. It has become a result.

When the only certain future is pollution all around us and the bomb overhead, secure links with the past, our feet on the ground, even thrust into the soil, are all the more important. We must feel traditions from our history, but not romantically, or on the precious assumption that everything was better once upon a time, so that the mechanical world ought to be destroyed.

Another acquaintance is a professor who spends every spare minute farming sheep out in the skerries. Burdensome at times, his farm is documented from the early sixteenth century, making him the most recent of a long line of farmers who have lived and worked there. He would regret being the last, the man who put it out of use, turned it into a sort of summer hobby, with the land finally leased out. Never!

Traditions bind him so strongly that the mere thought of selling confronts him with a hundred ghostly farmers staring accusingly at him: 'If you let these ditches fill again, allow the bushes to grow back over these fields, over this land that destroyed our backs—we should then have borne stones and farmed in vain...'

Unable to bear that, he struggles on.

Another acquaintance has bought a small farm in the farming south, in Skåne. He has a swimming pool behind the house, a washing machine and a hot shower in the former cart shed, even a sauna—but no water in the kitchen itself, just an enamel bucket and scoop, for that's what one has in the country, that's what he had in his childhood home, in fact. And do I need to say that his childhood home was painted red and had white-painted corners?

Near Katrineholm once, a hour or two south west of Stockholm, I came across a man in a sort of doctor's coat who was busy with the chickens outside his house. He proved to be a former managing director of a west-coast refinery, now a farmer and producer of goats' milk cheese. His new occupation was much better than the old, being in one way far better, for now he controlled his life, he thought. If it was cold he fetched in some wood and lit the stove. He had no need to ring OPEC first and ask if he had the means.

He used very little cash, the farm gave him most of what he needed. Although his case can hardly serve as an example for all Swedes, it is easy to understand him.

A little of that do-it-yourself, control-your-own-world, is to be found among Swedish pleasure fishermen, at least among those blessed with a summer *stuga* or some bothy in the country, or perhaps some attic in a summer place.

I don't know who he is, I see him only as a symbol for a Swede in summer. He has a woolly cap on his head, and he has a contour that suggests a high level of marginal taxation; perhaps he's a divisional director in some large group.

He has money enough to buy all the fish he needs, and a good wine to go with it. But he's going to catch the fish himself.

Nothing remarkable, really, many people like fishing, and this fellow must be driven by the same urges as any other pleasure fisherman in Europe or Japan (where one fishes in ponds merely for the pleasure of the catching), but I'd be prepared to bet he's driven by some other force, namely, to contribute to the housekeeping.

It's certainly fun to fish, to mess about with nets and boats and get up early and all that, but an essential part of it is that he can bring home something for the pot.

He has no need to keep an eye on his expenses. If he catches nothing he won't starve. It isn't that: but the non-economic contribution to the household provides the motive power. Yesterday we ate grilled Baltic herring, and the day before it was boiled perch-pike, and the day before that pike with horse-radish sauce and butter, while tomorrow we'll try the flounders and on Saturday herring done like gravlax...

Now if his company dining-room menu had looked like that our friend the fisherman would have commented, weightily, backed up by pin stripes, white shirt and wine thermometer. Here, however, in the country, where he goes about in overalls, a torn sweater and gestures with a pipe better used for boiling tar, here it is the fish that matters, for he, and no-one else, has caught it.

In other words, the comfortably-off summer Swede plays at being farmer or fisherman, growing his own salad, carrots, potatoes, catching his own fish, and pointing out that his vegetables are from his own ground, that he has no pecuniary need to do all this. He could buy the lot and not feel the cost.

Very well, one may say, OK, he thinks it's fun to putter about the garden and to fish, what's wrong with that?

Nothing at all. It isn't the least bit ridiculous to play at being a self-sufficient farmer/fisherman, and he's absolutely right that one's own salad and newly-caught fish taste better. The point is that the Swede has to weigh in the housekeeping aspects of his hobby.

It's a game, for if things go wrong and the crop is ruined, or if he loses a hook, he can put everything right with a visit to the nearest store. But it's still bloody serious, for he needs this self-sufficiency game as a bow to the past, to those vanished generations and their lives and way of living, their struggle on earth. This, undeniably, is why our friend the divisional director can stand in his comfy attic and muddle with a net, and at the same time honour his cautious hard-working predecessors. His game supports a tradition.

The net sinkers really ought to be stones: with holes in, or held in the complicated wooden frames used on Öland. Not a bit of rusty shock absorber from some deceased car, for all that it might do the job just as well. It wouldn't be at all the same.

WELL, NOW, LET'S LEAVE our friend the director with his net and return to The Swedish Home. As we now know, it shall be painted red, with the red paint from the Falu copper mine. The mine was once the largest in Europe.

The company that runs it today has recently taken the name of Stora—simply 'The Great'. This is less hubristic than it may sound, for the company began operations sometime in the thirteenth century. Some centuries later, it had occasion to order something or other from the USA. In ignorance of all this, the putative supplier sent back a discreet enquiry as to standing, credit and all that. The answer was that as the company had been doing business for some two hundred years before Columbus came across what became America, such nosiness was out of place: immediate delivery was what was wanted.

Farm *stugor* have not always been red: for a long time they were grey.

During the sixteenth century the roofs of palaces, big houses and churches were painted red. During Sweden's Great-Power period (1560–1718) the colour spread, so to say, to larger timber-built houses; their owners wanted to imitate brick.

When the houses of the better off began to be painted yellow, to imitate sandstone, red paint slipped down the social scale and began to be used on quite ordinary *stugor*. During the National Romantic Period, at the end of the nineteenth century (when Norway was

91

successfully getting free of the Swedish crown), red paint was being applied as never before: but production reached a peak in 1939, when 2359 tons were made. The works burned down in 1975. Having been rebuilt they now make about 1200 tons of pigment a year, or enough for 175,000 normal-sized farms.

The pigment consists of decomposed copper ore that contains silicic acid. It is purified, dried, burned and then mixed with boiling water, rye flour, and green vitriol; after more boiling it is ready for application. Falu red should be used fresh. Once upon a time people boiled it up themselves, often in a pot borrowed from the local church—the parish 'kettle'—and recipes varied infinitely. People threw in more or less anything: linseed oil, the liquid from pickling herrings, urine, resin, glue, soot, spruce bark, buttermilk, soap, carbon black.

The result was the red paint Swedes now associate with the Swedish landscape, a colour that is as fine against blindingly white snow as a dark coniferous forest or a field of golden-yellow rapeseed in flower.

Once linseed oil became an ingredient, the paint stopped rubbing off when touched. It manages at once to protect wood against rot and to permit moisture to escape, so that the wood can breathe. And it's durable: one needs to repaint only once every ten years.

The Swedish House having acquired its characteristic red, the commemorative songs began. "As we travel past little red *stugor*...," "We shall live in a little red *stuga*..." or, a little scandalously, in the parody of a song (known in the US as 'Bubbling Over'): "Off to plunder and throttle/With sword and oath and bottle/Gut with fire red *stugor*..."

IF YOU ASK SWEDES to name some typically Swedish things, they will reply *fatost* (a sort of cheese from Ångermanland), *surströmming* (fermented Baltic herring, from there, too), meat balls (less Swedish than Turkish, brought home by a Swedish king, who had been politely but firmly kidnapped by the Ottomans for some years), some variety of porridge, or something else strange to eat. Others might reply local-government music schools, the Workers' Educational Association (*ABF*, for short), or our crazy love of the formalities of associations.

Wielding the chairman's gavel is practically a national sport, along with fussing over the drafting of articles of association or a constitution, keeping, attesting, and then circulating minutes.

For my part, I'm prepared to acclaim as typically Swedish, both in the way it came into existence and developed, something that surely mirrors the whole of how we moved towards higher standards of living. A very special mixture of collectivism and individualism, tradition and new thinking, pioneering spirit and plegmatic comfort.

No Stockholmer will be puzzled by 'Årsta Beach' as a concept: a child's summer place, preferred before all others, for contact with nature, for bathing day after day, summer after summer. Foreigners, even out-of-town Swedes, may have much to learn.

Årsta Beach was started by *HSB*, the cooperative housing association, still going strong, at a time when comfortably-off Stockholm families—father, mother, children and a maid—would enjoy summers in rented houses, larger or smaller, somewhere in the skerries outside Stockholm. Families would wave off fathers from steamer piers in the morning and return there in the evening to welcome them back from a day's work in a practically deserted Stockholm.

Summer pleasures for uncomfortably-off Stockholmers were to be enjoyed rather nearer the city—in Essingen, for example, although, looking at its motorway, one is hard put to believe this.

Long, long ago, Essingen meant rented plots, small-gardens-with-stugor, (singular: a *kolonilott*), where vegetables and flowers could be grown, and whole days enjoyed, in summer. Intended only for garden things, such a *stuga* could accomodate surprisingly many people, but even this was barely a dream for the average Stockholmer. Living in cramped quarters and working long hours for poor pay, he and his family could only entertain fantasies of pleasant summers—and costly travel and high land prices made them even more hopelessly remote. Thoughts had already begun to circulate that town children ought to get out into the country in summer, but now grown-ups found themselves included in these ideas: sea bathing, relaxation and contact with nature became more and more important.

The authorities had previously only really been interested in the morals and conduct of those beneath them. Now they became aware of vassals with bodies that had needs of their own, for which sport and exercise had significance, and so on and so forth. *HSB* made a start: its architect-chairman, Sven Wallander, a distinguished member of a distinguished family, took his committee on a trip to the outskirts of Stockholm, looking for places in the skerries suitable for what they would unblushingly call the little people.

Some 30 kilometres from Stockholm they found a perfect area: a fine wood of conifers and deciduous trees backed what is unusual in the tideless skerries, a long sandy beach, on an arm of Hårsfjorden, where unknown submarines were so energetically hunted in the early 1980s.

It was purchased in 1929, for 250,000 *kronor,* and things could get started. Ten types of houses (*stugor*) were produced: all small and inexpensive, the least costly being 250 *kronor* down and 100 *kronor* a year for ten years, then 50 *kronor* a year for another five years. The site was leased, at 7 to 14 *öre* per square metre. The average area of 700 square metres would thus have cost 50 to 100 *kronor* a year. (In

1986 some people still pay at a rate of 8 *öre.*) There were to be 700 *stugor,* and those who wanted might build for themselves.

Within two years, each owner had to have encircled his plot with a fence of the sole approved design. In the square shops sprang up, almost as in a children's rhyme: butcher, baker, barber, grocer, haberdasher, fishmonger, greengrocer, tobaconist, photographer, post office, petrol station, and one of those very Swedish kiosks (newspapers, sweets, tobacco, and a long row of etceteras). *HSB* arranged its own timber yard, where do-it-yourself owners could buy the timber they needed. Lest the birds be disturbed by so much competing domesticity, *HSB* issued free nesting boxes. In addition, a large bathing place was built. *HSB* moved its pavilion at the 1930 Stockholm Exhibition to Årsta: it became, with additions, the hotel.

And little people streamed in to Årsta. Now they had real summer pleasures to look forward to, and Saturdays and Sundays throughout the year in the country. The enthusiastic Wallander donated, wholly or in part, things like tennis courts, a outdoor dance floor and bathing jetties.

It would have been impossible in any other country, but the social minister Himself, Gustav Möller, who held that post for some 22 years between 1924 and 1951, bought a *stuga* for himself and his wife, Else Kleen. Expressing some exquisitely Swedish sentiments, she wrote in a 1933 number of the *HSB* periodical, *Vår Bostad* (Our Dwelling): "Årsta Beach is the first attempt I know of to standardise and so make democratic the love of nature enjoyed by those poor Swedes who work in large cities . . . the first attempt made in our country to make nature really accessible in a democratic way for those people who don't otherwise have any possibility to get regularly out into the country."

The *stugor* at Årsta could be inherited, and could be bought and sold, too. *HSB* made heroic efforts to hinder speculation by a diversity of regulations of purchase prices.

There was neither running water nor lavatories in the *stugor,* but a water mains, shut off in winter, ran outside a few metres away, and one shared a dry closet with three or four others. *HSB,* of course, took responsibility for removing the necessary containers at regular intervals. Everything at Årsta was regulated by a paternal *HSB.*

Masses of events evolved: swimming and sporting competitions, regattas, swimming schools, gymnastics, Youth Days, thousands of others. Comprehensive arrangements for midsummer included every sort of traditional element: haycarts decked with leafy boughs, whole flocks of bowing and scraping fiddle players, dances, competitions, tombola and the rest. There were dances Wednesdays and Saturdays in summer. At the bathing place, while visitors paid, *stugor* owners showed a sort of identity tab and got in free. As one owner happened to be a Stockholm revue impresario, the Casino Revue paid an annual visit.

The whole area was alive with kids, thousands of them, all the teeming generations of the 1940s. The bushes were full of them, squabbling like sparrows.

As early as 1930 *HSB* had permission from the local council to open the shops on Saturdays and Sundays. The local pastor disagreed, holding that Sunday opening would detract from the tranquility of the day of rest and reduce attendance in church.

The sale of Class II Pilsner, one of the uneasy Swedish compromises between pure water and good beer, was forbidden in the shops, but not in the fully-licenced hotel. It was highly popular for a time as a venue for conferences.

This high-speed planning and building of a complete society is not unique in Sweden. The Stockholm Tramway Company planned the football stadium at Råsunda, north east of central Stockholm, so as to have somewhere to take people to in its trams. Both did very well.

At Årsta, little people inhabited little *stugor* on little plots and

96

PHOTO BY HANS FÄLTH, Träslövsläge

Swedish summer afloat: brush your teeth over the stern, piss over the bows,
and dive in amidships. One's summer licence runs from June to August.
{97}

PHOTO BY BIRGER LALLO, Vetlanda

Horses that time forgot, as they might have been in propaganda films for farmers' savings banks in the 1930s.
[98]

Swedish cock on Swedish dunghill: all part of the dream-world small-holding.
[99]

PHOTO BY MATS SANDSTRÖM, Norrköping

Something is eavesdropping on our tales of farmers ploughing behind horses, sowing by hand, nodding by the fire of an evening, while whittling teeth to a new rake.
[100]

Countryman with dog, uncontaminated by the romance that confuses urban heads when they consider rural life. As he rides a woman's bike probably for convenience, one may presume his home has TV, a video, other electrical essentials, and lots of plastic, also for convenience.
[101]

*Can there be anything finer than to dig exactly the quantity of potatoes
one needs for dinner from one's own land? This is potato growing on a
rather larger scale, or preparations for an unusually large dinner.*
[102]

*A well-laid reed roof will last thirty years, and those who possess the art,
like builders of tile stoves, are now no longer a threatened species.*
[103]

PHOTO BY JAN GRANATH, Staffanstorp

Nature, neat and tidy, in Skåne, after an early frost.
[104]

PHOTO BY INGEMAR BERGMAN, Nora

A lone walker in the fells, in pursuit of stillness, immense views, adventures, and a week's return to natural origins and subordination to nature's sway.
[105]

Abisko, Lappland, in autumn (= late August). Snow, having finally melted in June, is already back. Ice will shortly follow, and what will then happen to the crimson birch? Winter is never really absent here.
[106]

An ancient craft or art, traditional potteries and potters are part of what Swedes love about their past.
[107]

Pastural scene with elk, I: at rut, glittering with dew and belling out its breath in the early morning, an elk is something fabulous, like a newly awakened dragon in a child's tale.
[108]

PHOTO BY HANS BÖRJESON, Hammarö

Pastural scene with elk, II: most tales about elk are actually told by hunters, and end with a bang, while the elk, after a little hard work, ends in the freezer.
{109}

PHOTO BY ANITA LEVÉN, Luleå

In the depths of winter, Swedes keep off the powers of darkness with the help of an imported saint (Lucia), mulled spiced wine, and processional songs in day nurseries, schools, hotels, churches.
{110}

The Old City of Stockholm is medieval and, in winter sunlight and a blast of snow, looks it.
{111}

PHOTO BY FREDRIK LAUDON, Malmö

*Cold, desolate, bare and inhuman perhaps, but if there's copper to be dug,
someone will be induced to dig it and ignore the awful scenery. A view of
the Viscaria copper mine in Lappland.*
[112]

enjoyed a great sense of community. The many carless would bike out from town, or go by train and bus: they were one reason why a timber yard was arranged on the spot. People had their summer pleasure, but the new name, *sportstuga,* indicated a different attitude to summer holidays: they were for activity and exercise, walks and contact with nature. Still, even in the 1950s, we, the people of Årsta, had something in common with the plump bourgeoise who migrated to the skerries in summer: we, too, took along much of our worldy goods, although we had no maids. We took practically everything else: sheets, pillow cases, towels, blankets and mattresses, china and glass and cutlery, kitchen things and corkscrews—we took out to Årsta just about everything we had at home.

For my sister and me this was dreadful. Dad would attach to the back of Fido, our minute Fiat 500, something like a wheelless railway-station luggage cart of the time. On it would be strapped an enormous iron-bound trunk, heavy as sin, the whole car would be filled up with odds and ends, and food for the first few days, and then we were more or less off. The crux of the journey was the long hill on the Årsta Road up towards the Dalarö Road. We were convinced poor Fido would never make it. It was a relief when we could bike out with Mum, escape the awful tension, and so get our bikes out into the country.

Summer holidays were possible because mothers didn't work: fathers worked in town, and fathers with cars could commute. On Saturdays, for one worked on Saturdays then, fathers arrived about one o'clock, demanding coffee.

We carried water, cut wood, felled trees... went swimming in all sorts of weather, usually rain, played with legions of friends and returned home to town for the school term. Echoes in bare strange-seeming staircases heralded re-entry into town life.

Then the changes began. First the hotel went badly and didn't pay, its conferences dried up, summer-*stugor* people kept away, dance nights no longer drew the crowds, it closed. In the early 1960s, the local fire brigade set it professionally alight for the professional pleasure of putting it out.

Then welfare came, beginning with water: more and more people extended the mains into their *stugor*, but no-one worried much. We did it to avoid the need to go out and fetch water, which had meant a bucket and scoop in the kitchen, so it was alright to bring the water a little nearer, at first. And under *stugor* people had cement pipes, or simply holes in the ground, as cellars; trap-doors in floors provided access. Electricity came later, in the fifties, with refrigerators. The bolder even fitted water heaters and showers. Drains were dug. Private toilets—not water closets, for there were no such drains—but varieties of dry closets, were installed and the shared premises were abandoned. Now everyone has their own.

Cars were problematic as early as the later fifties, having once been absolutely forbidden on the narrow gravel paths within the main area; they had to be left some way off, in some proper place, and one then simply walked, carrying all one's bits and pieces, to one's *stuga*. The prohibition was finally withdrawn: we could drive up to our *stugor*. On some smaller plots, the cars seemed almost as large as the *stugor*.

TV aerials began to sprout in the early 1960s, and in the evenings Nature was left, unexpectedly, in peace. Ten years earlier, when TV had been under discussion, a Swedish professor fulfilled his oracular role to declare that the Radio Service, clucking over its little TV channel, had hatched a sickly chick. TV, the seer perceived, would be as nothing for Swedes whose devotion to sport, nature and association meetings would leave no time for it. Even a Swedish professor can misread the signs of the times.

Now we had electricity, and hot and cold water, and TV, and a car outside, but around us were wilting community events. Soon we had no Sports' Day, nor Youth Day with kids's parades, nor many other expressions of community.

Kids grew up, *stugor* aged, voices were heard proposing that plots might be bought outright, and sold, together with *stugor,* lock, stock and barrel. It was done: *HSB* has now transfered its interests to the owners' association. *Stugor* and fences must no longer be of approved patterns, and people are almost free to choose their own colours of exterior paint! An unprecedented phase began in Årsta's development: people bought and sold, tore down and altered, built anew and built bigger, but still within the maximum of 60 square metres.

Friggebo houses appeared. Long verandas and sun decks were sometimes so enthusiastically added that no more was left unbuilt than sufficed for a narrow boundary path.

The ultimate middle-class seal on this planned, collective dream was the building of a beach walk, with artifical lighting. This splendour was achieved partly through the removal of some seven thousand huge boulders: they had always been fun to jump about on, and to shelter between from the wind in cosy sun traps on fine days.

During these years the shops closed one after another, and if the cooperative Konsum remains, it occupies an ugly tin shed. The kiosk is still there, but nothing else.

Something else was beginning to happen: a renewed interest in the community, new sports events (including a mini-marathon). A combined bakery and lunch bar appeared in the square, and the old spirit began slowly to revive in new forms.

It was obviously time for a generational change. I recall my father bought our *stuga* for 5000 *kronor,* or a bit less than a year's pay, in 1953. Slowly but surely, as standards of living rose, we applied the principle of the second home to buy more and more things for the *stuga:* bedclothes, china, glass and cutlery, a little radio, and in the end a TV.

115

'Who would have believed,' said my father. 'That one day we would have two of everything!' He seemed almost shocked at the luxury and pomp of it all.

The kids of the 1950s began to take over the houses, and with them and their friends, something of the old spirit is back, a liking for doing things together coupled to an ambition to nuture the feeling that we do have roots in this society that *HSB* once upon a time quite simply conjured into existence. We may look like New Swedes, all us with our two cars and two TVs and video and ·electronics and all, but we are as small farmers were, eyes cocked for what the neighbours might be up to.

FOR SWEDES, AS I'VE SAID, Sweden is nature, but of what sort? One of the fine things about Sweden is its many different sorts of nature. One category of people is drawn to the fells in the north: meditative types, like Dag Hammarskjöld, lone wolves, adventurers, fishermen and many others. So far as I can see, the fells attract people because you can so easily die there.

Nature really is nature in the fells, not like it is in parks or fields or meadows, but the real indifferent thing that turns its back on mere people, its uninvited guests, and ignores their mighty self-importance, pays no heed to their capacities. The fells can orchestrate a storm without caring if people can dance to its music or not, freeze to death, or somehow manage to stumble back to their hotels.

Some people are most impressed by this, being otherwise used to the welcomes of agreeably neat and tidy forests, or to the greetings of well-clipped meadows, or the assurances of well-ploughed fields that docile nature works to benefit human beings.

116

Human beings are sovereign in such landscapes: in the south of Sweden they can stroll about over their country properties, but in the fells claims of ownership are absurb. Fences, where they exist, are to persuade reindeer to run in one direction rather than another, not to enclose a little plot of private land. Who would be so silly as to put up a four-cornered arrangement of personal fencing, to stand back and admire it, the work of one's hands!

A tourist in the fells is like the caliph in the Thousand Nights and the One Night, who clothes himself in rags and squeezes out through a tiny gate in palace wall to mix with his people, to learn what they think of him or of some rival potentate, but his real reason for this disguise is its danger. Tired of his monumental safety and the day-to-day luxury of his surroundings, he takes risks like drugs to challenge dangers. Sometimes accompanied by some massive faithful servant who can hold off over-close reality, he may sometimes risk being quite alone, exposed to the incalculable whims of his subjects.

And a visitor to the fells may do the same: leave his oil-fired house and, with a birch-bark pack of oranges and distress rockets, to set off to meet the elements, maybe even their rage.

His faithful servant will be someone at home on the hills since childhood: now a tolerant grown-up who lets him muddle about and make a fool of himself, drop his matches in a stream, break his fishing rod, forget the map, wander off anywhere but in the right direction, souse himself in the river and douse the spirit stove at mealtimes. And when everything is most dangerous and ensnarled he will produce from his enormous pack just what's needed to save the day.

The fells are interesting just because it really is so good to die there.

Travelling by car along one of the shallow valleys with a hundred and fifty miles to go and an outside temperature of minus 35 degrees Centigrade, one commonly meets no other vehicle, and is all the time only an engine failure from death by freezing. Alone in a nicely heated car, wearing slacks and a comfortable shirt and listening to the car radio: if the motor suddenly stops, warmth will very quickly seep away, perhaps as darkness gathers. That's to be alone in an undisturbed natural world. Getting out of his silent car, the shivering driver can look around at the fells and the snow and the trees, brilliant blacks and whites in the starlight and suddenly realise: all this nature doesn't give a damn for me, it hasn't even seen me.

Or on a nice day outing on skiis, a mile or so from the hotel with one's youngest son floundering about on wobbly legs in front: the wind suddenly increases, snow as fine as flour begins whizzing over the surface, the sun vanishes, so does the hotel, the boy begins whining that he's tired, skiis fall off all the time and can't be got to fasten, and the wind keeps on increasing . . . the fells are unlike anywhere else in Sweden.

Sometimes I stop and stand still and look at groups of houses on the South Side, or elsewhere in Stockholm: stare at them intensely, think them away, so to say, until they do vanish. In their place one sees, not without a stir of feeling, the grass and rock, the natural world, unrefined, as it was in the beginning, before the town spread out over it. This is to see the town as a brief episode, a temporary growth on the mocking eternal bedrock that here and there breaks surface.

That feeling is always present in the fells, together with the endless beauty of their untamed being: a mountain fox or a lemming, where a human being, left alone and naked, wouldn't survive twelve hours.

Anywhere else in Sweden, if you lose your way and wander about for ten or fifteen miles you'll run up against a house sooner or later, but in the fells there are only more crests behind the ones you can see. One might be an astronaut on the moon.

Perhaps one doesn't really travel to the fells to die: but then maybe the chance of doing so there is part of their attraction.

If the fells are wild then Öland, the slender Baltic island, where I have often been in summer, is the reverse: a friendly mild landscape, where Our Lord goes out every night to cut the grass in secret, where lovely juniper bushes stand everywhere in small groups like people chatting to one another at a party, where walls divide up the landscape and the sun shines even on rainy days. It is a secure landscape with the sea always present in the background.

In winter on land, snow is an obstacle and a trouble, it settles and makes a nuisance of itself. Snow in the fells is quite different, it fits in, as it were, as part of the landscape, giving the intense impression that nature, asleep, at rest, is living death, and oneself some unimportant guest in its realm, a disturber of its peace who dares to go about among sleeping birches and break their imperative silence.

In the fells you can get a heightened feeling of urgent environmental problems just because there is no visible sign of any destruction there. They are our correlation.

So has it been from the beginning. Oh mankind, what have you done?

'A gloomy people, much given to merriment,' my citation from Hjalmar Söderberg, a writer compared to Joyce, is a good motto: it sums us Swedes up, and illustrates my dilemma. Fumbling after characteristics of a whole people one finds nothing but contradictions, every statement calls up its opposite. Perhaps the only safe thing to say is that we live where we do. In Sweden, a wonderful country.

*